VOCABULARY
START-UPS

by
Murray Suid

illustrated by
Mike Artell

Publisher: Roberta Suid
Editor: Annalisa McMorrow
Cover Design: David Hale
Design & Production: Scott McMorrow

Other books of interest include:

*Thinking Start-Ups, Writing Start-Ups, Ten-Minute Grammar Grabbers,
Ten-Minute Editing Skill Builders, How to Be President of the U.S.A.,
Cooperative Language Arts, Cooperative Research & Reports,
Book Boosters, Storybooks Teach Writing*

For a complete catalog, write to the address below:

Monday Morning Books
P. O. Box 1680
Palo Alto, CA 94302

Or visit our World Wide Web site:
http://www.mondaymorningbooks.com
e-mail: mmbooks@aol.com

ISBN 1-57612-003-1

Printed in the United States of America

987654321

Contents

INTRODUCTION

The English language contains about a million words. More are added daily. No one can hope to learn them all. However, using the strategies found in *Vocabulary Start-Ups*, everyone can engage in the fascinating, lifelong odyssey of building a bigger and better vocabulary.

THE ACTIVITY CARDS

This book contains scores of activity cards printed two to a page. Each card presents a mini-lesson dealing with one or more of the following topics:

• etymology
• grammar (parts of speech)
• meaning
• pronunciation
• spelling
• structure (syllables, prefixes, suffixes)
• type of word (homonyms, abbreviations, acronyms)
• word references (dictionary, glossary, thesaurus)
• writing style (cliches, word choice, imagery)

Each card introduces the topic with a brief definition. Next, a quick **Try this** activity provides hands-on experience. These activities involve such tasks as brainstorming ("List ten important proper nouns in your life"), analyzing ("Break these words in syllables"), or defining ("In your own words, explain the meaning of the interjections *aha* and *hmm*").

The "Try this" activities generally take less than ten minutes. Some require the use of a dictionary, such as the *Macmillan Dictionary for Children*. Because etymology is an element in many lessons, you might wish to reproduce the list of
etymologies found on pages 82 through 84.

Each card also includes a follow-up **Extra** that encourages students to apply the knowledge they've acquired, for example, by writing homograph riddles or inventing memory tricks for spelling words. These tasks can be done in class or for homework.

USING THE CARDS

The cards can be used in three ways. To set up an **independent vocabulary building program**, duplicate and laminate the pages on card stock. Some teachers like to use one or more colors. Cut the cards apart and place them in a shoe box or other container.

Give the class a brief overview of how the cards are structured. You might suggest that students enter their work in a "Vocabulary Notebook." The reproducible "Activity Log" on page 80 will enable students to keep track of their efforts. Answers to selected exercises appear on pages 89 through 95.

For **large group instruction**, simply choose a card yourself and copy it onto the chalkboard. You'll also find a collection of whole class Teaching Extensions on pages 74 through 79.

A third option is to use the cards for **at-home study**. In this case, each student will choose a card and copy the activity into his or her notebook.

WHERE TO START

Because word acquisition is a nonlinear process, there is no one right place to begin. For this reason, the lessons appear in alphabetical order. You might start with the A's and work through the cards in ABC order. Another approach is to choose topics for specific units, for example, word origins, spelling, or parts of speech.

RESOURCES

You can give additional practice by using the lists at the back of the book. These include: tongue twisters, pronunciation puzzlers, idioms, homograph riddles, and eponyms.

The Reading List presents children's books on a variety of topics, such as puns, etymology, and spelling.

BEYOND THE BOOK

We welcome your questions and comments. Write us at:

Monday Morning Books
P. O. Box 1680
Palo Alto, CA 94302

Or visit our World Wide Web site:
http://www.mondaymorningbooks.com
e-mail: mmbooks@aol.com

ACTIVITY CARDS

Abbreviations

An "abbreviation" is a shortened form of a word or phrase. For example, *Dec.* is the abbreviation of December. Usually, an abbreviation ends in a period.

Let's do an abbreviation operation.

Try this: Write the long form of the following abbreviations. If you're not sure, use the dictionary.

- Dr.
- Jr.
- Mrs.
- Inc.
- Mr.
- A.M.

Extra: Abbreviations are used in many jobs and activities. For example, in chess *P* stands for *pawn*. Pick an activity that you know about, and list at least three abbreviations that are used in it. Explain what each one means.

Acronyms

An "acronym" is a word made from the first letter, or letters, of other words. An example is *NASA*, which stands for <u>N</u>ational <u>A</u>eronautics and <u>S</u>pace <u>A</u>dministration.

What does it mean?

Try this: Use a dictionary to find the words represented by the following acronyms.

- radar
- sonar
- scuba
- UNICEF

Extra: Create an acronym using the letters in your name. For each letter, find a word that describes you. For example, "Elke" might choose the words "<u>E</u>nergetic, <u>l</u>ikable, <u>k</u>ind, <u>e</u>ducated."

Adjectives

An "adjective" is a word that adds meaning to a noun (a naming word). For example, in the phrase "a squeaky clarinet," *squeaky* is an adjective.

Try this: List at least twenty adjectives that say something true about you. Each one should fit in the blank in the sentence: "I am_____." For example, "I am smart."

Extra: Look through a dictionary and find five adjectives you never knew before. They may be marked with the abbreviation *a.* or *adj.* Include the meaning with each adjective you list. For example, *precise* (exact).

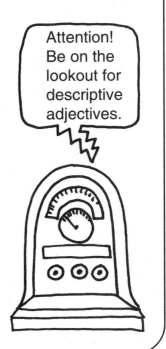

Attention! Be on the lookout for descriptive adjectives.

Adverbs

An "adverb" is a word that adds meaning to a verb (an action word). For example, in the sentence "The dog ate quickly," *quickly* is an adverb that describes how the dog ate. Many adverbs end in *ly*.

Try this: List five actions that you do every day. Each one should fit in the blank in the sentence: "I _____ every day." Then match an adverb to each verb. For example, if one of your verbs is *giggle*, you could match it with the adverb *frequently.*

Extra: In a dictionary, find five adverbs. Write a story or essay using one of those adverbs in the title.

I drink quickly, too!

Advertising Words

An "advertisement" is an announcement that tells the benefits of a product. Because space to publish is costly, ad writers try to make every word count.

Baby sitter available for weekend work...

Try this: Write a 25-word advertisement to sell one of the following items.

- your school (why should kids want to go there?)
- a service (for example, baby-sitting)
- an event (for example, a play)

Extra: Make a poster showing advertising tricks. These include: claims ("We're number 1!"), emotional words ("family"), repetition ("free, free, free"), and catchy rhymes ("Jake's Shakes").

Alliteration

When two words start with the same sound, that's called "alliteration." For example, the "b" sound is repeated in the phrase "beach ball."

Many monkeys mean more mischief.

Try this: List five words that describe you. Then turn at least two of them into alliterative phrases. For example, if one word is *fast*, you might create the alliterative phrase "fabulously fast." Use one of your phrases as the title of a story or poem.

Extra: Collect at least three examples of alliteration. You can often them in poems, songs, newspaper headlines, and product names.

Alliterative Names

Story writers sometimes give their characters alliterative names. A famous example is Bugs Bunny.

My story is about a daring detective.

Try this: Create an alliterative name for at least two characters. Think about:
• someone who likes to climb or swim
• a friendly snake
• a wealthy villain
• a strong horse

Extra: Make up alliterative nicknames for at least three people you know. Include yourself.

Anagrams

An "anagram" is a word made from all the letters of another word. For example, *stop* is an anagram of *tops*. So is *pots*.

Try not to gape at this page.

Try this: Find an anagram for each of the following words. In some cases, there will be more than one anagram.
• ear   • hint   • tools
• peal   • redo   • care

Extra: List at least three words that have anagrams. Then challenge people you know to figure out an anagram for each word.

Anagram Riddles

An anagram riddle is a sentence with two missing anagrams. The words in the sentence act as a clue for the anagrams. In this example, the broken lines tell how many letters the anagrams have

I drink _ _ _, when I _ _ _ cookies.

A heart <u>beats</u> in the chest of this mighty <u>beast</u>!

Try this: Write an anagram riddle for each of the following anagram pairs. Then test the riddles on people you know. If no one can guess the riddles, rewrite them to make them easier.

• owl, low • adobe, abode (*abode* means *home*)

Extra: Create an anagram riddle book. Put one riddle on a page. If you like, add picture clues.

Antonyms

An "antonym" is a word that means the opposite of another word. For example, *hot* is the antonym of *cold*. Words with several meanings may have several antonyms. The antonym of *hard* (meaning "firm") is *soft*. The antonym of *hard* (meaning "difficult") is *easy*.

I make <u>smiles</u> out of <u>frowns</u>.

Try this: Find an antonym for the words below. In some cases, the antonym can be a two-word phrase.

• old   • helpful   • noisy
• expensive   • always   • careful

Extra: *Button* has no antonym. List five other words that have no opposite.

Back Formations

When a noun is turned into a verb, the new verb is called a "back formation." For example, the verb *sculpt* came from the noun *sculpture*. *Sculpt* is called a back formation of *sculpture*.

Try this: Find the noun that was the source of each verb below by completing the sentence.

• Someone who burgles is called a _____.
• If you scavenge, you're a _____.
• If a show is televised, it's seen on _____.

Extra: One way to turn a noun into a verb is to add the ending *-ise* or *-ize*. Add *-ise* or *-ize* to *cable* or *laser* to create a new verb. Then use it in a sentence.

Do you think they'll televise the Big Game on television?

Blended Words

A "blend" is a word formed from part of one word and all or part of another word. *An example* is *smog*, which a blend of *sm(oke)* and *f(og)*.

Try this: Find the words that were blended to form the following words. It's OK to look them up in a dictionary.

• brunch   • motel   • splatter

Extra: Create a blend. Start by imagining a new thing that combines two older things, for example, a *robot* that acts like a *bat*. Then figure out how to blend the two old words, as in *robat*.

Mix up a batch of blended words.

Borrowed Words

Many English words were first used in other languages. When you look up a word, some dictionaries tell you where it came from. They also give the word's spelling and meaning in that language. For example, the word "bomb" came from the Italian word *bomba*, meaning "loud noise."

Carpenter comes from the French *carpentier*.

Try this: Find the language or country from which each of the following words came.

- boomerang
- chipmunk
- kilt
- centaur
- fiord
- reveille

Extra: Trace a world map and show where these or other borrowed words came from.

Borrowed Word-hunt

There are about a million words in English, more than any other language. That's because English has borrowed words more often than any other language.

Try this: Choose a room at school or home. List at least ten words that name things in the room. Then use a dictionary to find which languages the words came from. You may need to use a special dictionary.

Gather borrowed words like a bee gathers honey.

Extra: Write a report about a language that English borrowed many words from. These include French, Spanish, Italian, and German.

British English

English varies from place to place. For example, a *thumbtack* in the U.S. is a *drawing pin* in England.

Try this: On a seperate piece of paper, match the English and American terms.

Nappy is British English for *diaper*.

American Terms		British Terms	
bangs	flashlight	accumulator	fringe
battery	French fries	chips	lift
elevator	checkers	torch	draughts

Extra: Write a story or essay using British words. Others include: dustbin (garbage can), crisps (potato chips), and constable (police officer).

Buzz Words

A "buzz" word is a new word or phrase that becomes popular. It might be the name of an invention, a place, or a person. A recent example is the *World Wide Web*. Often people aren't sure what a buzz word means, even though "everyone" is using it.

Write down some buzz words of the future.

Try this: Use your imagination to visit the distant future. Think up amazing inventions and activities. Then make up at least three buzz words that might be used by people living in that time.

Extra: Report on a few buzz words of the past by interviewing an adult or reading old newspapers.

Cliches

A "cliche" is an overused word or phrase. Examples are *special* and *Have a good day*. Cliches usually are boring. That's why careful writers and speakers try not to use them.

"Don't touch that dial; more cliches are coming right up."

Try this: Rewrite the following sentences without using the underlined cliche.

- It was <u>raining cats and dogs</u>.
- That movie was <u>out of this world</u>.
- <u>Last but not least</u>, I want to thank my cousin.
- I was nervous, but you were <u>cool as a cucumber</u>.

Extra: List at least five cliches that appear on television, on the radio, or in books.

Cliche Catching

We get so used to cliches, we sometimes don't even notice them.

Reel those cliches in like a fish on a line.

Try this: List all the cliches that you find in the following paragraph.

I got up on the wrong side of the bed this morning. My mom said, "Turn that frown upside down." Then she added, "This room is a pig sty. I want to see it clean as a whistle." I did what she asked, quick as a flash. It was easy as pie."

Extra: Find a different way to communicate each of the cliches that you found in the paragraph.

Clipped Words

Many words are shortened or "clipped" from longer words. For example, *photo* was clipped from *photograph*. In some cases, a word was was clipped from two words. For example, *principal* (head of a school) came from *principal teacher*.

Ref is clipped from the word *referee*.

Try this: For each word, find a shorter word that was clipped from it. It's okay to use a dictionary.

- omnibus
- airplane
- pantaloons
- taxicab
- submarine
- examination

Extra: List a word or phrase with two or more syllables, for example, elephant. Create a clipped word by leaving out a letter or several letters.

Coined Words

Usually, there's no record of who first used a word. But sometimes, a scientist, an inventor, or a writer will invent a new word. This is called "coining a word." For example, in 1967, a writer working for a clothing company coined the word *dashiki* as a name for a loose-fitting, brightly colored robe.

Blimps can fly, and so can I.

Try this: Use a dictionary to find the name of the people who coined the following words.

- blimp
- blurb
- gas

Extra: Think up an idea for an invention or a new sport or activity. Describe it, and coin a word to name it, for example, a "thwarp."

Colloquial Language

Daily speech is called "colloquial." It is less formal than language used by scientists and other professionals. For example, the formal word *masticate* has a colloquial synonym, *chew*.

Feline is a formal way of saying *cat*.

Try this: Find a colloquial word or phrase that matches each of these formal words. Use a dictionary if you like.

- askew
- analyze
- enlist
- essential
- expenditure
- throng

Extra: Find formal words to match the colloquial ones below. You can use a dictionary or encyclopedia.
- skin
- tears (crying)
- food

Compound Words

A "compound word" combines two other words, for example, *classroom* (*class + room*). Each word in a compound must be able to stand alone. For example, *television* is not a compound word because *tele* is not a separate word.

Daylong comes from the two words, *day* and *long*.

Try this: For each word below, find a compound word that includes it.

- ball
- eye
- note
- door
- book
- head
- side
- high

Extra: Find at least ten compound words in a book or newspaper. Divide each one to show the two words it was made from.

Compounding

Joining two words to make a compound word is the most common way of creating new words in English. This is called compounding.

Try this: Find at least ten compound words in the dictionary.

Extra: List at least five objects that you see or use every day. Examples might include a pencil, paper, and a comb. Imagine a new way to use each item, or a way to improve it. Then give the object a new, compound-word name. For example, a bicycle powered by the sun might be called a "sunbike."

A robot with wheels might be a "wheelrobot."

Conjunctions

A "conjunction" is a word that joins words or groups of words. Examples include *and*, and *when*.

Try this: Copy each example on a piece of paper. Follow each boldfaced conjunction with words to form a complete sentence.

• I will smile **if**_____.
• The cat wanted to come in, **but**_____.
• Let me have the book, **or**_____.
• We'll go swimming, **unless**_____.

Extra: Find five conjunctions in a book or in a newspaper. Write the phrase or sentence containing each conjunction and underline each example.

I can read *or* watch TV.

Connotation

"Connotation" refers to the personal meaning of a word or phrase. For example, to many people, the phrase "used car" has the connotation of "trouble." That's why some car dealers use the label "pre-owned car," which they think gives a more positive feeling.

You can *clown around*, or you can *have fun.*

Try this: Replace the underlined words with words that mean the same thing but that have more positive connotations. It's okay to use the dictionary.

• <u>cheap</u> gift   • <u>skinny</u> person   • a <u>miser</u>

Extra: Choose one of the following words and write a few sentences that give your connotation of it.

• summer   • shopping   • math   • homework

Consonants

"Consonants" are the speech sounds represented by the following letters: *b, c, d, f, g, h, j, k, l, m, n, p, q, r, s, t, v, w, x, y, z.* Some consonant letters represent different sounds. For example, *s* makes one sound in words like *sip* and a different sound in a words like *his.*

Salmon has a silent l.

Try this: Find words that show the two sounds made by the following consonants. For example, "c" makes an "s" sound, as in "city." It's Ok to use a dictionary.

• c   • g   • x.

Extra: Consonants are sometimes silent letters. For example, *k* is silent in *know*, and *b* is silent in *debt.* Find three other examples of silent consonants.

Contractions

A "contraction" is a word formed by omitting letters from a word or phrase. For example, *he'd* is a contraction of *he would*. An apostrophe (') marks where the missing letter or letters used to be.

You'll find contractions everywhere.

Try this: Give the original word or phrase from which these contractions were made.

- can't
- I'll
- we're
- wouldn't
- you're
- five o'clock

Extra: Collect at least five examples of contractions used in advertisements, books, songs, or other kinds of writing.

Contraction Making

Contractions make writing seem more natural. This works well in friendly letters. For example, instead of "I will be there," you could write, "I'll be there."

Try this: Write the following words or phrases as contractions. Be sure to include apostrophes.

- she will
- they are
- did not
- could not
- are not
- I would

I'd rather run than swim.

Extra: Pretend you're a newspaper editor and must shorten two headlines. Do it by inventing two new contractions. Contract the underlined words. Remember to use an apostrophe.

- <u>Computer</u> Prices Fall
- Mission to <u>Jupiter</u>

Dialogue Tags

When characters speak in a story, their words are called the "dialogue." Writers tell readers who is talking by using dialogue tags such as *he said* and *she laughed*.

Try this: Complete the dialogue tag for each of the following examples:

- "Quiet, I hear them coming," she _____.
- "What is the strange light?" he _____.
- "You'll be sorry," she _____.

Extra: Make a report on the dialogue tags used by a favorite writer. Skim a chapter or two in a novel and list the different dialogue tags that you find.

Digraphs

A "digraph" is a combination of two letters to represent a single sound. For example, the letters *ph* in *graph* represent the sound of *f*. The *ea* in *sea* represent the sound of *e*.

Try this: Name a single letter represented by each underlined digraph in the following words:

- lau<u>gh</u>
- <u>wh</u>ale
- h<u>ee</u>l
- <u>sc</u>ience

Extra: To catch attention, ad writers sometimes replace digraphs by inventing new spellings. An example is replacing "you" with "u" as in "U-Store-It." Find three examples in signs around your town.

Echoic Expressions

"Echoic" words imitate natural sounds. Examples include *crash*, *gurgle*, and *hiss.*

Try this: Think about a typical day in your life, from the time you get up until the time you go to sleep. List as many echoic words as you can that could be used to describe the activities during the day.

Extra: Write and illustrate a picture book that presents echoic words of interest to little kids. Examples are *zoom*, *ding-a-ling*, and *moo.*

Ruff, ruff, ruff...

Echoic Names

The names of many products are echoic. For example, a bottled water company might name its product *Glug-Glug* to imitate the sound that water makes as it pours.

Try this: Think up an echoic name for each of the following products.

- a new kind of cereal
- athletic shoes
- an airline
- a carbonated drink

Extra: The names of many products found in supermarkets or advertised on television are echoic. Make a list of those that you know.

My secret spy company is called "Shhh."

Enunciation

"Enunciation" is clarity of pronunciation. Good enunciation is important to teachers, salespeople, singers, and others who want to be understood. The opposite of good enunciation is "mumbling."

Try this: Improve your enunciation with tongue twisters. Don't rush. Say the words as clearly as possible. After repeating a tongue twister three times without mistakes, go a little faster.

- Books build big brains.
- Should shadows shake?
- Rockets roar.
- Can crocodiles cry?

Extra: Create your own tongue twister. Start most of the words with the same sound. Have a partner test it.

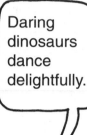

Daring dinosaurs dance delightfully.

Epithets

An "epithet" is a descriptive name or title. An epithet can describe a person, such as Peter the Great. Or it can describe a place, such as:

"America <u>the Beautiful</u>."

Try this: Create epithets for three people that you know. An epithet could relate to any aspect of the person's life including appearance, job, or hobby, for example, Murray <u>the Map Reader</u>.

Extra: Create an epithet for your school. Share your idea in a letter to the school paper.

XJ7, the world's greatest robot.

Eponyms

An "eponym" is a person or character for whom a place or an organization is named. For example, George Washington is the eponym of Washington D.C.

Rome was named for the mythological character, Romulus.

Try this: Find the eponyms (people) that the following places were named for.
- America
- Hudson Bay
- Bolivia
- Columbia

Extra: Pick a thing or a place that was named for someone. It could be a school, town, state, country, club, or product. Write a short report about the person.

Etymology

An "etymology" is the history of a word. It tells where the word came from. For example, *bank* comes from an Italian word *banco*, "bench." Long ago, bankers did business out of doors on benches. Some dictionaries include the etymology for every word.

Medicine can be traced back to the Latin word, *medicina*.

Try this: Find the following words in a dictionary. Write their etymologies.
- astronaut
- caterpillar
- ballot
- muscle

Extra: Find the etymology of your first name or the etymology of a word that interests you.

Euphemisms

A "euphemism" is a word or phrase that is less direct than another expression. For example, instead of calling someone a liar you might say, "You're not telling the truth."

Try this: Write a euphemism for each underlined expression. In some cases, you may need to use several words to get across the idea.

- Your room is a <u>mess</u>.
- I <u>lost</u> your watch.
- I'm <u>angry</u>.
- You <u>stole</u> my hat.

Extra: Write a report about a euphemism used in an advertisement.

Monkey business is a euphemism for silly behavior.

Exaggerations

To make a point, speakers and writers sometimes use words that stretch the truth. For example, a sportscaster might say that a player did "the impossible." Because no one can do what's impossible, the statement is an exaggeration.

Try this: Use a dictionary to find the actual meaning of the following words, which are often used to exaggerate something.

- amazing
- awesome
- miraculous
- fabulous

Extra: Report on one or more exaggerations used in newspaper ads, TV commercials, or everyday talk.

To *run like lightning* is an exaggeration for running very fast.

Foreign Words

When a word that comes from another language still sounds foreign, it should be underlined or written in italics. An example is the Russian word *nyet*, which means "no."

Did you know that the French word for *pencil* is *crayon*?

Try this: Use a dictionary to learn the meaning of the following foreign words used in English. Also find out what language each word comes from.

• cosmonaut   • bon voyage   • ciao

Extra: List five English words that you think would be of interest to people around the world. Explain why you think these words are so important.

Gender-free Words

"Gender" refers to whether a person is male or female. Because most jobs can be done by males and females, words such as *waitress* are being replaced by gender-neutral titles, such as *server*.

I'm happy to be a fish catcher!

Try this: Find a gender-free word for at least three of the following jobs.

• busboy   • meter maid   • salesman
• mailman   • policeman   • stewardess

Extra: Some people think that we should find gender-free words to express ideas like *brotherhood* and *man-made*. Write an essay that gives your opinion.

Gerunds

A "gerund" is a noun (name word) made from a verb (action word). Gerunds always end with the suffix *-ing*. For example, the gerund *throwing* is made from the verb *throw*.

Try this: List five gerunds that name activities you care about. For example, if you like to dream at night, your list might start with *dreaming*.

Extra: Pick a favorite character from a book, movie, comic strip, or TV show. List at least five gerunds that relate to the character. Then write an essay comparing the character's gerunds with those from your life.

Flying is the gerund formed from the word *fly*.

Given Names

A "given name" is the name a person gets at birth or baptism. In English, it's a person's first name, for example, *Julia* or *Juan*. Most given names have a meaning. For example, *Robert* comes from two German words meaning "bright fame." Given names are often chosen to honor a relative or famous person.

Try this: Write an essay telling why you were given your name and what the word means. You might use a dictionary or reference book of names.

Extra: Report on the given name of someone you know, for example, a family member or friend.

My given name is *Barney Bee*.

Glossary

A "glossary" is a kind of dictionary that defines words on a specific topic. In a baseball glossary, *strike* means "miss the ball." In a bowling glossary, *strike* means "knock down all the pins."

Try this: Choose a hobby or subject that you know about. Write a ten-word glossary that defines each word as used in that activity.

Extra: Create an imaginary glossary that would be read by one kind of animal. In a glossary for cats, *mouse* would have a different meaning than in a regular dictionary. Define at least five words.

My *bark* is different from tree *bark*.

High-tech Words

"High-tech" refers to computers, robots, lasers, and other up-to-date inventions. Although some high-tech words are totally new—for example, CD-ROM—others are old words given new meanings. For example, long before electronic computers were invented, the word *computer* meant "a person who could do arithmetic."

Try this: Give the old meaning and the high-tech meaning of the following words.
• hardware   • mouse   • net

Extra: Make a glossary of several high-tech words such as *laser, e-mail, modem,* and *virtual reality.*

I won't eat a *computer mouse.*

Homographs

"Homographs" are two words that are spelled alike but have unrelated meanings. For example, one word spelled *trip* means "to fall" and another word spelled the same way means "a journey."

Finding homographs can be fun!

Try this: Show the two meanings of the following homographs by writing two sentences. If you don't know the two meanings, use a dictionary.

• batter   • loaf   • tire   • bill

Extra: Homographs can have two pronunciations. *Bow* (to bend at the waist) rhymes with *cow*; *bow* (a weapon) rhymes with *go*. Use rhymes to show how to pronounce the two meanings of *bass*, *lead* and *wind*.

Homograph Riddles

A "homograph riddle" is a sentence with two blanks to be filled by a missing homograph. A clue follows each blank. For example:

Can you solve this riddle?

> "While you watch the _____(female pig), I'll _____ (scatter) the seeds in the garden.
> The answer is the homograph *sow*.

Try this: Create your own homograph riddle using one of the following homographs. If you're not sure what the two meanings are, use a dictionary.

• seal   • tire   • loaf   • spell

Extra: Write a homograph riddle book. You might use art to help readers guess the homographs.

Homonyms

A "homonym" is a word that sounds the same as a different word. For example, "toe" is a homonym of "tow." Another name for "homonym" is "homophone."

Try this: Find a homonym for at least four of the following words. Check them in a dictionary.

- bare
- here
- to
- right
- stair
- mined
- lone
- whole
- red

Extra: Homonyms, such as *its* and *it's*, cause spelling problems. Create a poster that warns spellers to be careful when using homonyms. Include examples.

Did you hear the *tale* about the dinosaur's *tail*?

Homonym Riddles

A "homonym riddle" is a riddle whose answer is a pair of sound-alike words. For example: What do you call someone with a basement shop? A cellar seller.

Try this: Figure out these homonym riddles. The answers are printed at the bottom of this card.

a. What are the cuttings in a bunny barber shop?
b. What do you call a jetliner that has no frills?

Extra: Write your own homonym riddles using the following homonym pairs or other homonyms that you know about: doe/dough; one/won; right/write; sea/see; son/sun.

Answers: a. hare hair, b. plain plane

The *two* of us like to skip rope, *too*.

Hyphenated Words

A hyphenated word is made of words joined by a hyphen (-), for example, a *loud-barking* dog. These words can turn into compound words. For example, *skyscraper* once was spelled sky-scraper.

Try this: Form at least three hyphenated words using words in each group. You can use a word more than once.

Group A		Group B	
good	soft	boiled	looking
hard	well	known	natured

Extra: Find five hyphenated words in a newspaper, book, or dictionary.

Fun-loving clowns make people laugh!

Hyphenation Editing

It's easy to forget to write the hyphen between words that should be hyphenated.

Try this: In the paragraph below, find four word groups that should be hyphenated.

On the twenty third of June, our family will drive our broken down truck to a seldom visited park. We'll pitch our blue green tent and tell nightmare causing tales around the campfire.

Extra: Invent a hyphenated word that describes you. Use it in the title of your autobiography, for example, "The Pizza-loving Painter."

Hard-working students will find the hyphenation mistakes.

Idioms

An "idiom" is a phrase that says one thing, but means something else. If you have "butterflies in your stomach," that means you're nervous.

You've hit the nail on the head means you're exactly right.

Try this: Imagine that you're teaching someone to speak English. Explain the meaning of these idioms. It's <u>raining cats and dogs.</u>

• My friend was <u>jumping for joy</u>.
• While on my bike today, I <u>had a close shave</u>.
• I can't talk because I'm <u>tied up</u> with other things.
• Don't <u>beat around the bush</u>. Tell me what happened.

Extra: Keeps your <u>eyes peeled</u> for idioms that you read or hear. Make a poster about them.

Infinitives

An "infinitive" is a phrase formed by combining *to* with a verb. For example, *to go* and *to sing*. You can use an infinitive to talk about an activity, as in the sentence "I like *to cook*."

I know how *to catch* really big fish!

Try this: List infinitives that describe five of your skills. Each should complete the sentence:

I know how _____.

You may add an object for the verb, for example, "I know how to build *models*, to hit *a baseball*, and to multiply *fractions*.

Extra: List infinitives that name skills you plan to learn: "Someday, I'll know how _____."

Initial Words

"Initial words" are made from the first letters of words or syllables. To pronounce an initial word, say the name of each letter. For example, E.T. ("extraterrestrial") is pronounced "Eee Tee."

BBC stands for the British Broadcasting Corporation.

Try this: Write the words which these initial words stand for. It's OK to use a reference.

- C.O.D.
- P.E.
- U.N.
- TGIF
- UFO
- TV

Extra: List at least three initial words found in newspapers and in advertisements. Tell what the initials represent. For example, UCLA stands for "University of California, Los Angeles."

Interjections

An "interjection" is a word that expresses emotion. For example, *wow*, is used to show excitement. Interjections are often used in writing dialogue ("Fe, fi, fo, fum"), cartoons and comics.

Eureka, I have found it!

Try this: Explain the meaning of four or more of the following interjections. Write a sentence to illustrate how the interjections are used.

- aha
- hmm
- nah
- yeah
- boo
- huh
- ouch
- yikes

Extra: Interjections make good titles, for example, Louis Phillips' *Oops!*, a book of mistakes. Use an interjection as a title for a story, poem, or essay.

Invented Spelling

In most kinds of writing, spelling errors annoy readers. However, advertisers sometimes deliberately misspell words to grab attention, for example, a cereal named KRUNCH.

Write Time Printing Company

Try this: Turn the following misspelled product names into correct English.

- Kwik Kleeners
- Koffee Kup Kafe
- Minit Kar Wash
- Sooper Soap
- U Stor It Lockers
- E-Z Eye Kare

Extra: Look for an example of an invented spelling business name in your town. Write to the owner asking why he or she decided to misspell the name.

Irony

"Irony" means using words to communicate the opposite of their usual meaning. For example, if you fall in the mud and say, "That's nice," you really mean "That's horrible." Advertisements often use irony: "Don't you love it when the phone stops ringing just before you pick it up?"

Banging my thumb is tons of fun!

Try this: Use at least three of the following words in a way that makes the words ironic.

- fun
- glad
- great
- wonderful
- easy
- smart

Bonus: Write a commercial that includes an example of words used in an ironic way.

Jabberwocky

"Jabberwocky" is a language of nonsense words.

Those words sure sound funny.

Try this: Explain the underlined words from Lewis Carroll's "Jabberwocky." There is no one right answer.

'Twas <u>brillig</u>, and the <u>slithy</u> <u>toves</u>,
Did <u>gyre</u> and <u>gimble</u> in the <u>wabe</u>;
All <u>mimsy</u> were the <u>borogoves</u>,
And the <u>mome</u> <u>raths</u> <u>outgrabe</u>.

Beware the <u>Jabberwock</u>, my son!
The jaws that bite, the claws that catch!
Beware the <u>Jubjub</u> bird, and shun
The <u>frumious</u> <u>Bandersnatch</u>!

Extra: Write your own gibberish-filled poem. See if readers can understand the nonsense.

Jargon

"Jargon" is the language of a special group. For example, baseball jargon includes *bunt* and *homer*. Words like *blastoff* and *orbit* are space jargon. Almost every job or activity has its own jargon.

Rod and *Reel* are fishing jargon.

Try this: Pick a topic you know a lot about. It could be a hobby, a school subject, a club, a sport, or any other activity done by a group. List at least five words that are part of the jargon of that activity, and explain each word in a sentence.

Bonus: Ask a worker to teach you some of the jargon used in that person's job. Make a report about this jargon.

Kin Words

Some of the most important words label family ties. For example, *brothers* names the relationship between two male children who have the same parents.

Sometimes *siblings* make the best friends.

Try this: Define these family words. Compare your definitions with those found in a dictionary.

- aunt
- brother-in-law
- cousin
- grandparent
- niece
- nephew
- step-father
- uncle

Extra: Research more unusual kin words. These include *sibling, second cousin, second cousin once removed, half-brother,* and *great uncle.*

Ladder of Words

"Specific" words point to one thing. For example, the word "Chicago" points to one city. On the other hand, "general" words refer to many things. For example, *city* refers to thousands of places. Words can be arranged like a ladder, moving from specific to general.

Animal, Dog, Collie, Lassie.

Try this: Rearrange the words in each group below to make a ladder with the most general word on top.

- game, checkers, activity
- apple, food, fruit, pippin

Extra: Create a word ladder that includes your name, plus words such as *student, human being, citizen of* _____ (fill in the name of your country), and _____ *grader.*

Manner Words

Although actions often speak louder than words, words can be a good way to show thoughtfulness.

Thank you for not clowning around.

Try this: Imagine that you're teaching English to someone. Explain each of the following expressions. When possible, give synonyms.

- Excuse me.
- No problem.
- Thank you.
- I'm sorry.
- Please.
- You're welcome.

Extra: Write a picture book of manner words for little kids. You might present the ideas in dictionary form or as a story. When you're finished, read the book to a young person.

Metaphors

Sometimes a word that names one thing is used to name something new that looks or acts like the old thing. An example is using *eye* to name the opening of a needle. This new use is called a "metaphor."

I am the wind.

Try this: Find a word used as a metaphor in each sentence. Use the word to show its first meaning.

- Please go to the head of the line.
- His house is located near the fork in the road.
- My speech needs some polishing.

Extra: In a sentence, use one of these words as a metaphor. Then use the word in its first sense.

- head
- star
- steps
- flipped

Nicknames

A nickname is an informal name for a person, a place, or a thing. Examples include *Bill* (William), Beantown (Boston) and *Old Faithful* (a geyser). Nicknames are often given in fun, for example, calling a very tall person "Shorty."

The *wireless* is an old nickname for the *radio*.

Try this: Invent an unusual nickname for the main character of a story. Then write the story about that character.

Extra: Collect or invent at least three kinds of nicknames. They can be based on the following:
- age
- hobby
- appearance
- job
- skill
- shortened form of a name

Nouns

Words that name people, places, and things are called "nouns." Nouns that name people include *artist*, *neighbor*, and *teacher*. Examples of place nouns are *bank*, *home*, and *school*. Thing nouns include *book*, *cloud*, *horse*, *money*, and *trees*.

Dinosaur is a noun, and so is *stegosaurus*.

Try this: List at least thirty nouns that name people and things in the room where you're sitting right now.

Extra: In addition to naming people, places, and objects, nouns can name ideas, for example, *friendship*. List three nouns that name ideas which are important to you, and explain why they matter.

Old-fashioned Words

Words can become old-fashioned. This can happen if people use a new word, for example, *car* instead of *horseless carriage.* In other cases, a thing loses its popularity, for example, *stovepipe hats.*

Alchemist is an old-fashioned word for chemist.

Try this: In a sentence, tell what you think these old words mean, then check them in a dictionary.

- icebox • rogue • parlor • pillory

Extra: CD players have become so popular, the word "phonograph" may soon sound as old-fashioned as "horseless carriage." Write an essay about something used today whose name may sound old-fashioned a century from now.

Onomatopoeia

"Echoic words" imitate natural sounds. Examples include *buzz*, *crash*, and *pow*. Using such words in poems, stories, and other forms of writing is called "onomatopoeia." An example would be naming a pet store "The Meow and Bark Shop."

Try this: Use onomatopoeia to name each of the following businesses:

- barber shop • plumbing repair
- car repair • toy store

I'm a bee that likes to *buzz*!

Extra: Write a story with a title that uses onomatopoeia, for example, "Roar!"

Oxymorons

An "oxymoron" is a phrase made of words that seem to be opposites. An oxymoron makes people think about the subject in a new way. For example, "After I spoke, there was <u>deafening silence</u>."

Don't act like a *big baby*.

Try this: Match words from the two columns to create sentences with oxymorons.

Column A	Column B
You're clearly...	insult.
I quickly...	honest.
That's a polite...	slowed.
He's unbelievably ...	confused.

Extra: Use an oxymoron in a story or a poem.

Palindromes

A "palindrome" is a word or phrase that is spelled the same forwards and backwards. Examples include *eve* and *level*.

Hi, I'm *Bob*, the *radar* robot.

Try this: Write down at least five palindromes in the following story. See if you can add other examples.

Just before noon, my friend and I told mom we'd take the baby for a walk. That's what we did. The baby wore a hat that was redder than the sun. It caught the eye of a passing bus driver who shouted "Wow!" and gave her horn a toot as she drove by.

Extra: Write a story, essay, or poem that uses palindromes and have a partner try to find them.

People Words

A "people word" is a word based on someone's name. Often the person isn't famous, but did something famous. For example, the saxophone is named for its inventor, Antoine Sax.

Seattle is a city named after a Native American.

Try this: Use a dictionary to find the names of the people behind these words.

• diesel   • pickle   • leotard   • volt

Extra: Dream up an invention and use your first or last name to name it. Write a paragraph that gives the story of the word.

Phonetic Spelling

Dictionaries include "phonetic spellings" that tell how to pronounce words. The phonetic spelling for *phonetic* is "fo NE tik." The *NE* is capitalized because that syllable is spoken with more force.

My friends call me "Roo fuss."

Try this: Write the phonetic spellings of these words. Note: Different dictionaries use different phonetic spellings.

• circuit   • gnome   • yolk   • Wednesday

Extra: Write your name using phonetic spelling. For example, one way to phonetically spell Monique is "mo NEEK."

Prefixes

A "prefix" is a syllable placed in front of a word or a syllable to makes a new word. For example, placing *re*, meaning "again" before *use* gives reuse.

Try this: Combine the prefixes with the words to make six words found in the dictionary. You can use a prefix more than once.

Review past games to learn from mistakes.

Prefixes		Words	
• il-	• pre-	clear	lease
• im-	• re-	legal	spell
• mis-	• un-	heat	mature

Extra: On your own or using a dictionary, write definitions for the prefixes *il-*, *pre-*, and *un-*.

Prefixes That Count

Some prefixes indicate quantity. For example, *mono-* means "one," as in *monorail*, "a one-track railway."

Try this: Match a number prefix on the left with a word on the right to form another word.

A *bilingual* person speaks two languages.

Number Prefixes		Words	
• bi-	• milli-	angle	cycle
• centi-	• tri-	meter	grade

Extra: Write another word using each prefix above and give its definition. It's OK to use a dictionary.

Pronouns

A "pronoun" replaces a noun. In the sentence, "My brother saw himself in the mirror," *himself* is a pronoun. Pronouns are used to avoid repetition such as "My brother saw my brother in the mirror."

Try this: Rewrite each sentence using a pronoun in place of the underlined noun or noun phrase.
• Because my dog barks, my neighbor hates <u>my dog</u>.
• After I collect the cans, I'll recycle <u>the cans</u>.

Extra: Pronouns can make interesting titles. An example is *Them!*, the name of a famous science fiction movie. Write a story, article, or poem using *It, We, You,* or another pronoun for the title.

My owner wants me to play with *her*.

Pronunciation Puzzlers

Many words are not spelled as they're pronounced. For example, in the word *sword*, the "w" is silent. The word is pronounced "sord."

Try this: Try pronouncing the following frequently mispronounced words. Then check yourself using a dictionary. Practice each word you missed
• adjective • debt • gnu
• epoch • vehicle • zoology

Extra: In a book, find three words that you're not sure how to pronounce. Look them up in a dictionary and write their phonetic spellings.

Write has a silent *w*.

Proper Nouns

A "proper noun" is the name of one particular person, place, thing, or product (a brand name). Proper nouns are usually capitalized. Examples are *Napoleon*, *Martha Washington*, *Rumpelstiltskin*, *Chicago*, *Oz*, the *Titanic*, and *New South Wales*.

Sherlock Holmes is a famous, fictional detective.

Try this: List at least ten proper nouns that have meaning for you. Include the names of people, places, and products. Be sure to capitalize each one.

Extra: Choose one of the proper nouns you listed above. Write a story or essay about the person, place, or thing named by that noun. Tell why the subject is important to you.

Pseudonyms

A "pseudonym" is a made-up name used to hide a person's true identify. For example, Poor Richard was Ben Franklin's pseudonym. A writer's pseudonym is sometimes called a "pen name."

Psst! Did you know that "Miss Manners" is really Judith Martin?

Try this: Make up a pen name for yourself. It might relate to a skill or experience that you have. For example, if you like to fish, your pseudonym might include the word *hook* or *water*.

Extra: Give the real names of the people behind these pseudonyms. Use a dictionary or reference book. Include one fact about each person.

• Lewis Carroll • Mark Twain • Dr. Seuss • O'Henry

Puns

A "pun" is the humorous use of words that sound alike or that have two meanings. For example:

> What did the potato chip say to the cracker?
> "Shall we go for a dip?"

In this riddle pun, "dip" means "going for a swim" and also "a thick sauce eaten as an appetizer."

Trees and dogs both love a good bark.

Try this: Explain the two meanings in this pun.

> What did the pony say to the throat doctor?
> "I'm a little hoarse."

Extra: Create a pun riddle using a word with two meanings or a sound-alike pair such as *pail/pale*, *shoe/shoo*, or *dear/deer*.

Questions

Newspaper reporters build stories around six questions: *who*, *what*, *where*, *when*, *why*, and *how*. These words are also used in other kinds of writing. For example, mystery stories are called "whodunits" because they focus on "who?" A book about a scientific discovery might focus on "how?"

Try this: Think of an incident in your life, and write a short article about it. In the article, answer the six questions:

- who
- what
- when
- where
- why
- how

Extra: Write a story, an essay, or a poem that uses a question word as its title, for example: "Why?"

Rebuses

May +  - e = Maybe

A rebus is a piece of writing in which pictures replace some words. For example, a picture of an eye can replace the word "I." A word can also be replaced by a picture plus a letter. For example, a picture of a heart plus "y" is "hearty." And "somer" plus a picture of a salt shaker equals "somersault."

Try this: Translate the following sentence into a rebus. Replace each underlined word with a picture or a picture plus a letter.

> From a <u>window</u> in my <u>house</u> <u>I</u> <u>can</u> <u>watch</u> the <u>sun</u> set each day.

Extra: Write a rebus picture book for little kids.

Reduplication

"Reduplication" means making a word by repeating part of an old word. For example, *chitchat* comes from *chat*. Both words mean "an informal talk" but *chitchat* has a funnier sound. Reduplicated words can also rhyme, for example, *willy-nilly*.

I like the pitter-patter of teeny-weeny feet.

Try this: In a dictionary, find the meaning of at least three of these reduplicated words.

- mishmash
- palsy-walsy
- flip-flop
- teeny-weeny
- ticky tacky
- pitter-patter

Extra: Write a story in which one character has a habit of using reduplicated words.

Rhyming

A "rhyme" is a pair of words ending with the same sound, as in "rhyme time." Rhymes are used in song, poems, titles, stories, and slogans.

Try this: Write an autobiographic rhyming poem. Begin by listing words that have meaning for you, for example, *soccer*, and *math*. Then find one or more rhymes for each word, (*soccer, locker, blocker*). Finally, use some of the rhymes in a poem that describes you.

Extra: Create a children's picture book that uses rhymes to tell a story. It could be an original story or one based on an old fairy tale.

Is that a clown frown?

Rhyming Riddles

A riddle with a rhyming answer is called a "hink pink." For example, what do you call a container shaped like an automobile? A car jar.

Try this: See if you can figure out the rhyming answer to the following riddles.

• What do you call a not fancy jetliner?
• What do you call an overweight bonnet?
• What do you call a library robber?
• What do you call a melody that lasts for an hour?

Extra: Create a book of rhyming riddles. Start by choosing rhymes and then writing clue sentences.

What do you call a large feline? A fat cat.

Rounds

A "round" is a definition game that takes the reader from one word to another to another and finally back to the first word. For example:

> What's a *bike*? A bike is a two-wheel vehicle.
> What's a *vehicle*? A vehicle is a tool for moving.
> What's *moving*? Moving is going somewhere.
> What's *somewhere*? Somewhere is a place.
> What's a *place*? A place is where things are kept, for example, a *bicycle*.

Try this: Write a round with five or more steps.

Extra: Gather a few partners and perform your round as a mini-play.

Slang

"Slang" is very informal language. Some slang expressions are old words used in a new way. An example is "cool" meaning "good." Because slang is often unacceptable in school, on the job, and elsewhere, being able to translate slang into standard English is a useful skill.

Try this: Replace the slang with non-slang words.
• The firefighter had <u>guts</u> to enter the burning barn.
• I <u>ain't</u> going with you.
• That's a <u>cool</u> shirt you have on.

Extra: Write a report about slang that people no longer use. For research, try interviewing an adult.

Sniglets

Some everyday things don't have their own names. An example is the awful noise made by chalk on a chalkboard. A "sniglet" is a made-up word or phrase that names such nameless things.

Try this: Name at least one of the following items.

- fog that you breathe out on a cold morning
- a drawing made on a dusty car fender
- a shrunken bar of soap that's too small to use
- the bit of "stuff" left after you use an eraser

Extra: Find something that needs a name, and name it. Tell about your word in an article or letter sent to your school or town newspaper.

What sound does a robot make when it thinks?

Spelling Patterns

If a verb ends in a silent *e* (*give*, *save*), the *e* is dropped before adding *ing* (*giving*, *saving*). If you pay attention to this kind of pattern, you may become a better speller.

Try this: Describe the pattern for each group.

- cry/cries, fry/fries, dry/dries, fly/flies
- bat/batted, rip/ripped, tap/tapped
- happy/happier, silly/sillier, sloppy/sloppier

Extra: When *i* and *e* are found together in a word, the *i* usually comes first. But *eight*, *freight*, *rein*, and *weigh* all have the *ei* letter order. Write a paragraph that describes this pattern.

At work, I *operate* on an *operating* table.

Spelling Tricks

A "spelling trick" is a sentence that helps you remember how to spell a difficult word. It uses a simple clue word found inside the tricky word. The sentence "I ride the <u>bus</u> to the <u>bus</u>iness area" can help you recall that *business* starts with "b-u-s."

Try this: Find a clue word inside four or more of these words.

- forty
- often
- hoarse
- believe
- been
- early
- instead
- separate

Extra: Write a spelling trick sentence for one or more of the words above. The sentence should contain the clue word and the longer word.

Suffixes

A "suffix" is a syllable added to a basic word to change the word's meaning. For example, "ly" changes the word *friend* to *friendly*.

Extra: Write the basic word by dropping each suffix. For example, *musical* becomes *music*. Then define each suffix yourself or with a dictionary.

- musical
- finalize
- youngster

Extra In your own words, explain the meaning of each underlined suffix and use it in another word. Check your definition by looking in a dictionary.

- fly<u>er</u>
- help<u>ful</u>
- good<u>ness</u>

Surnames

A "surname" is a family name. In English-speaking countries, surnames come last, but elsewhere family names come first. Many surnames originally referred to things such as a color (Green), a person (Johnson = John's son), or an object (Hammer).

My name is Bill *Carpenter*.

• **Try this**: From among your friends, neighbors, and characters you read about, find an example of each of the following kinds of surnames:

- place
- color
- object
- job
- animal
- time

Extra: Write a report on the meaning of your surname or the surname of one of your heroes.

Syllables

A "syllable" is a word or part of word said all at once. *Bat* and *May* are one-syllable words. *Batter* and *April* have two syllables. Recognizing syllables can help you spell and understand words.

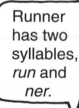

Runner has two syllables, *run* and *ner*.

Try this: Say the following words to yourself and break them into syllables. Use a dictionary to see if you found the right places to break the words.

- computer
- exaggerate
- metric
- dozen
- intelligent
- concentration

Extra: Common words usually have fewer than four syllables. But some words have more. Find three words in the dictionary with at least four syllables.

Syllable Simplification

A simpler word for *feline* is *cat.*

Good writing usually includes short and long words. However, because short words are easier to read, writers often use short words when writing safety signs or stories for young children.

Try this: Replace the following words with words that use one or two syllables. You might need to use several shorter words to replace a longer word.

• automobile   • education   • pedestrians

Extra: Write a paragraph describing a person or activity, but use only one-syllable or two-syllable words.

Syllable Stressing

Clowns are *FUN ny.*

In words with two or more syllables, usually one syllable is spoken louder ("stressed"). Dictionaries identify the stressed syllable either with capital letters (FARM er) or an accent mark (farm' er).

Try this: Say each word aloud and write the stressed syllable with capital letters or an accent mark. Compare the results with those in a dictionary.

• carrot   • flashlight   • mistake   • telephone

Extra: Collect ten two-syllable words. Then write a report telling which syllable is usually stressed in a two-syllable word.

Synonyms

A "synonym" is a word that means almost the same as another word. Synonyms are useful because they let writers avoid repetitions. For example, instead of writing "I saw a *huge* rat that was so *huge* it scared me," you could write "I saw a *huge* rat that was so *enormous* it scared me."

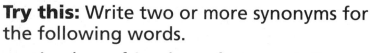

My *friend* and I are best *pal*s.

Try this: Write two or more synonyms for the following words.
• animal • friend • fast • talk

Extra: Read a newspaper story and find at least two synonyms used to avoid repeating the subject.

Thesaurus

A "thesaurus" is a book of synonyms (words with similar meanings) and antonyms (words with opposite meanings). A sample entry might be:

> **happy** (synonyms): cheerful, glad, contented, joyful, lighthearted
>   (antonyms): dejected, gloomy, unhappy, sad

Writers use the thesaurus to avoid repeating words.

A synonym for *book* is *tome*.

Try this: Make your own thesaurus entry for these words. Write at least three synonyms and three antonyms for each word.
• big • smart • brave

Extra: Compare your words with those in a thesaurus.

Time Words

Like air, water, and food, time plays an important role in every person's life. No wonder there are so many time words.

Try this: Briefly explain the following time words.
- second
- hour
- week
- season
- minute
- day
- month
- year

Extra: Write a story that takes place during one of the time periods listed above. Or use an unusual period such as one of the following. You may want to check the word's meaning in a dictionary.
- fortnight
- nanosecond
- millennium

Fishing *season* is the time of year to fish.

Trademarked Names

Just as you can own things, you can own a product name. It's called a "trademarked name." An example is "Astroturf." No one else can use that name for similar products. Trademarked names are usually capitalized. Often they are followed by the symbol ™.

Try this: Describe the kind of product represented by these trademarked names. For example, "Astroturf" is a kind of fake grass.
- Band-Aid
- Frisbee
- Kleenex

Extra: Create an original name for a product such as a jump rope. Tell why you think it's a good name.

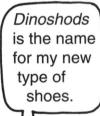

Dinoshods is the name for my new type of shoes.

Two-way Words

When you read a "two-way word" backward, it's a different word. For example, *net* backward is *ten.*

Try this: Create a few riddles using two-way words. For example: "With my butterfly ____, I caught ____ butterflies." Use the following two-way word pairs, or find your own examples:

- am/ma
- brag/garb
- lap/pal
- pots/stop
- rats/star
- on/no
- part/trap
- flow/wolf
- smart/trams

Extra: Write a book of riddles featuring two-way words. The introduction should include an example. Answers can go upside down or on the next page.

Umbrella Words

An "umbrella expression" is a word or phrase that includes or "covers" specific words. For example, *workers* covers many jobs such as *carpenter*, *dentist*, *electrician*, *soldier*, and *teacher*.

Try this: For each of the following umbrella words, list five words or examples that fit under it.

- buildings
- foods
- places

Extra: Pick an umbrella word that's important to you, for example, *friends* or *favorite*s. Then list words or examples that fit under it.

Verbs

A "verb" is a word that describes the action in a sentence. For example, in the sentence "The rocket roared into space," *roared* is the verb.

Try this: Write a sentence that includes five actions you have never done but would like to do someday. Underline each verb. For example, your sentence might begin, "Someday, I will <u>sky-dive</u>, <u>read Chinese</u>..."

Extra: In a dictionary, find three verbs that are new to you. Write their definitions.

Visual Words

Ad writers, sign makers, and poets sometimes letter words in a way that shows their meaning. The result is a "visual" word. For example:

```
      um
   b     p
```

Try this: Use unusual lettering in a way that shows the meaning of at least three of the following words. Or choose your own words.

- curve
- flat
- slanted
- stairs
- squeezed
- tall
- tangled
- thick

Extra: Make a report about visual words that you found in newspapers, billboards, or other places.

Vowel Pairs

An old rhyme says, "When two vowels go walking, the first vowel does the talking." This means that if two vowels are together in a syllable, they make the sound of the first vowel's name. For example, in *bait*, the *ai* is pronounced like the name of the vowel <u>a.</u>

Radio ends with an EE O sound.

Try this: In the sentence below, list the words that follow the rhyme and those that don't.

> Please read me the book about the sailors whose boat floated across the sea on a journey to buy bread and beans.

Extra: Find at least three more words that follow the rhyming rule about vowel pairs.

Word Root: aster

The root "aster" is from a Greek word meaning "star," as in *aster*, a star-shaped flower. A related form of the root is "astro," found in *astronaut*, a person who flies into outer space.

Try this: Write the definitions of at least six of the follow words. It's OK to use a dictionary.

- asterisk
- asteroid
- astral
- astrocompass
- astrodome
- astrolabe
- astrology
- astronomy
- disaster

Extra: Russian space explorers are called *cosmonauts*. Briefly explain the root "cosmos" and list at least one other word that grew from it.

Word Root: biblio

The root "biblio" is from a Greek word meaning "book." An example is *bibliotheca*, a synonym for library.

Try this: Use a dictionary to find the meaning of the following "biblio" words.

- Bible
- bibliography
- bibliomania
- bibliophile

Extra: The root of *library* is the Latin word "liber." Give the meaning of this root.

Word Root: bio

The root "bio" comes from a Greek word meaning "life." You find this root in many words, including *biography*, which is the study of a person's life.

Try this: Use a dictionary to find the meaning of at least three of the following "bio" words.

- autobiography
- biopsy
- biography
- biology
- bionics
- biometrics

Extra: Because of recent discoveries in biology, many new "bio" words have appeared. These include *biodegradable*, *bioethics*, or *biofeedback*. Write a short report on one of them.

Word Root: cap

The root "cap" comes from a Latin word meaning "head." Two articles of clothing—*cap* and *cape*—probably grew from this root.

Try this: Use a dictionary to find the meaning of at least four of the following "cap" words.

- capital
- capsize
- capitol
- capitalism
- captain
- capitalize

Extra: *Capture* comes from a different root from the one meaning "head." Use the dictionary to find what it is. List one other word that relates to *capture*.

Word Root: chron

The root "chron" comes from the Greek word for "time." This root is found in *chronicle*, a record of events. *Chronicle* has been used as a newspaper name, for example, *The San Francisco Chronicle*.

Try this: Use a dictionary to find the meaning of at least three of the following "chron" words.

- anachronism
- chronic
- chronometer
- synchronize

Extra: A *chronology* lists events by date or hour. Write a chronology of your life. List five or more important events, for example, the first time you rode a bicycle.

Word Root: dict

The root "dict" comes from the Latin word meaning "to speak." You'll find this root in the word *dictionary*.

Try this: Use a dictionary to find the meaning of at least three of the following "dict" words.

- dictator
- indicate
- predict
- diction
- indict
- verdict

Extra: Another Latin root—"voc"—means "voice." It's the source of many English words, for example, *vocal*. Find another "voc" word in the dictionary.

Word Root: dyna

The root "dyna" from a Greek word meaning "power." It's found in the word *dynamite*.

Try this: Use a dictionary to find the meaning of the following "dyna" words.

- dynamic
- dynasty
- dynamo

Extra: Write a short report on an invention whose name is built on the "dyna" root. Choices include *dynamite*, *dynamo*, and *dynamometer*.

Word Root: geo

The root "geo" comes from a Greek word meaning "the earth." For example, *geology* is the study of the earth's crust, rocks, and fossils.

Try this: Use a dictionary to find the meaning of at least two of the following "geo" words.

- geography
- geocentric
- geothermal
- geometry

Extra: The study of the moon's crust is called *selenography*. Write a short report that tells the etymology of that word.

Word Root: graph

The root "graph" is from an ancient Greek word meaning "to carve." Later, it meant "to write" or "to draw." In the nineteenth century, "graph" was combined with the Greek word for light to make *photograph*.

Try this: Use a dictionary to find the meaning of at least three of the following "graph" words.

- autograph
- cardiograph
- graphology
- calligraphy
- graphics
- paragraph

Extra: An *autobiography* is the life story of the person writing the story. Write your autobiography in about one hundred words.

Word Root: ject

The root "ject" comes from a Latin word *jacare* meaning "to throw." For example, a *conjecture* is a guess made by "throwing ideas together."

Try this: Use a dictionary to find the meaning of at least two of the following "ject" words.

• inject   • project   • object   • reject

Extra: The word *jet* also traces back to the Latin word *jacare*. Read about jet engines and then write a report on how the invention relates to the idea of "throwing."

Word Root: legis

The root "legis" comes from a Latin word meaning "law." The root is found in the word *legislator*, a person who makes laws.

Try this: Use a dictionary to find the meaning of at least two of the following "legis" words.

• illegal   • legislature
• legal   • legitimate

Extra: Write a short report giving the roots of two words that relate to lawmaking: *congress* and *parliament*.

Word Root: manu

The root "manu" comes from the Latin word for "hand." You'll find it in many words, for example, *manacles*, which means handcuffs.

Try this: Use a dictionary to find the meaning of at least four of the following "manu" words.

- manicure
- manual
- manufacture
- maneuver
- manners
- manuscript

Extra: The word *digital* comes from a Latin word that relates to the hand. Write a short report giving the root of the word *digital* and its meaning.

Word Roots: mis/mit

The roots "mis" and "mit" come from a Latin word meaning "to send." For example, a *missile* is something that is sent into space.

Try this: Use a dictionary to find the meaning of at least three of these "mis" and "mit" words.

- admission
- omit
- dismiss
- permit
- mission
- remit

Extra: The prefix "mis-" has a different meaning from the root "mis" in the above words. Find the meaning of the prefix "mis" and list three words that begin with it.

Word Root: mot

The root "mot" comes from a Latin word meaning "to move." The root is found in *motile*, a word used to describe something that can move on its own.

Try this: Use a dictionary to find the meaning of at least three of the following "mot" words.

- demotion
- motion
- motive
- emotion
- motivate
- motor

Extra: Explain how the word *automobile* relates to the root "motus."

Word Root: ped

The root "ped" comes from an ancient Latin word meaning "foot." A similar root *pod* is found in the Greek language.

Try this: Use a dictionary to find the meaning of at least four of the following "ped" words.

- biped
- pedal
- pedicab
- pedicure
- peddler
- pedometer
- expedite
- pedestal
- podiatrist
- impede
- pedestrian
- tripod

Extra: The letters *ped* in *pediatrician* and *pedagogy* come from a root that has nothing to do with foot. Using a dictionary, tell how these words are related.

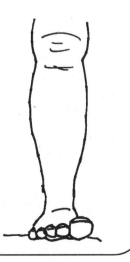

Word Root: pel

The root "pel" comes from a Latin word meaning "to push." When you *compel* someone to do something, you push the person to do it.

Try this: Use a dictionary to find the meaning of two of the following "pel" words.

- expel
- propeller
- propel
- repel

Extra: In some words, the root "pel" is changed to "pul." Find the definitions of two of these words: *pulse* and *propulsion*.

Word Root: philo

The root "philo" comes from a Greek word meaning "love." A *philosopher* is someone who loves knowledge.

Try this: Use a dictionary to find the meaning of two of the following "philo" words.

- philanthropist
- philodendron
- philharmonic
- philology

Extra: The root "philo" is found in the city name, *Philadelphia*, meaning "brotherly love." Write a report on the etymology of the name of your town or city. This might involve telling who or what the place was named for.

Word Root: phono

The root "phono" comes from a Greek word meaning "sound" or "voice." It is found in the word *telephone*.

Try this: Use a dictionary to find the meaning of at least three of the following "phono" words.

- microphone
- phonology
- phoneme
- phonograph
- phonics
- sousaphone

Extra: Another Greek root is "photo." Write a short report giving the meaning of "photo" and give at least two words that grew from it.

Word Root: port

The root "port" comes from an ancient Latin word meaning "to carry." For example, a *porter* is someone who carries baggage or other things.

Try this: Use a dictionary to find the meaning of at least four of the following "port" words.

- deport
- export
- important
- report
- deportment
- import
- portable
- transport

Extra: The word *port*, which means *harbor,* comes from a different Latin root. It's the same root found in *porthole*. Give the meaning of this other "port" root.

Word Root: rupt

When a water main breaks, we say that the pipe ruptured. The root of that word is "rupt." It comes from an ancient Latin word meaning "to tear."

Try this: Use a dictionary to find the meaning of at least three of the following "rupt" words.

- abrupt
- erupt
- corrupt
- interrupt
- disrupt
- irrupt

Extra: Look up the etymology of *reap* and explain how this word relates to the root "rupt."

Word Root: script

The root "script" is from a Latin word meaning "to write." It's the source of the English word *script*, meaning "the words of a play." In some words, the letters of the root change, with *p* replaced by *b*.

Try this: Use a dictionary to find the meaning of at least three of the following "script" words.

- description
- scribble
- inscribe
- scribe
- manuscript
- scripture

Extra: A *scroll* is a rolled paper or parchment with writing or pictures. Look up *scroll* in a dictionary to see if it came from the root "script."

Word Root: sect

The root "sect" comes from an ancient Latin word meaning "to cut." For example, at an *intersection*, one street cuts the other.

Try this: Use a dictionary to find the meaning of at least three of the following "sect" words.

- bisect
- insect
- sector
- dissect
- section
- vivisection

Extra: Guess why the root "sect" is found in *insect*. Then check the etymology in the dictionary. In a paragraph, explain the connection between "sect" and "insect."

Word Root: sign

The root "sign" is from a Latin word meaning "a mark." When you sign your name, that's your *signature*.

Try this: Use a dictionary to find the meaning of at least three of the following "sign" words.

- design
- signal
- designate
- signet
- insignia
- significant
- resign
- signify

Extra: People are sometimes asked to sign a petition. But what is a petition? Briefly give the word's meaning and its root.

Word Root: tele

The root "tele" is from an ancient Greek word meaning "distant." This root is found in the name of many inventions, such as television (seeing far off).

Try this: Use a dictionary to find the meaning of at least four of the following "tele" words.

- telecast
- telegraph
- telephoto
- telegram
- telemetry
- telescope
- telephone
- telepathy

Extra: Imagine a new invention for sharing information at a distance, for example, studying with a teacher without actually being there. Coin a name for your invention using the root *tele*.

Word Root: tract

The root "tract" comes from a Latin word meaning "to pull." A *tractor* is a vehicle used to pull farm machinery.

Try this: Use a dictionary to find the meaning of at least two of the following "tract" words.

- attraction
- retract
- detract
- traction

Extra: Like the tractor, many means of transportation have interesting etymologies. Give the etymologies of at least three of the following words: *bus*, *helicopter*, *jeep*, *parachute*, *submarine*, and *trolley*.

Word Root: viv

The root "viv" comes from the Latin word meaning "to live." This root is found in many words, such as *survive*, meaning "to continue to live."

Try this: Use a dictionary to find the meaning of at least three of the following "viv" words.

- revive
- Vivian
- vivacious
- vivid

Extra: The root "vit" is a relative of "viv." You find it in the word *vitamin*. Write a short story about vitamins and explain what the word has to do with "life."

X Words

When *x* starts a word, it usually makes the sound of the letter *z*. An example is *xylophone*. The only exceptions to this rule are the word *x* meaning "to cross out" and hyphenated words such as *X-ray*. These exceptions begin with the sound "eks."

Try this: In a dictionary, find the meanings of at least two of the following X words.

- xenon
- Xerxes
- xi
- xenophobia
- xerography
- xylem

Extra: The letter *x* is a symbol used in several ways. For example, it can stand for a person's name. Find at least two other meanings of the letter *x*.

I have *xanthous* colored fur.

You

The word *you* is commonly used in everyday speech, when one person talks to another or to a group. In writing, *you* is important if the writer wants to create a close tie with the reader. This is often done in friendly letters, advertisements, and directions.

You might find me living in a jungle.

Try this: Write directions that teach a reader how to do something, for example, ride a bike. Use the word *you* in the directions.

Extra: As a way of drawing readers into a story, use the word *you*. For example, "You're walking down a dusty road. To your right is an old barn. You hear strange music and stop to listen."

Zillions of Numbers

Number words play an important role in many activities, such as business and science.

Humans use only a *fraction* of their brains.

Try this: On your own, define each of the following words or phrases. Then compare your definitions with those of the dictionary.

- decimal
- digit
- even number
- fraction
- metric system
- odd number
- one
- zero

Extra: Write a children's picture book that explains one or several number words.

Resources

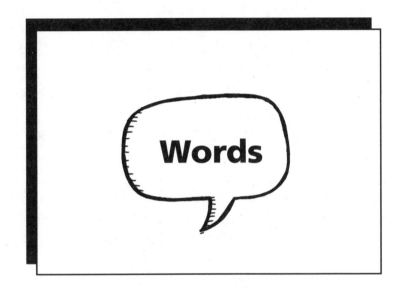

Teaching Extensions

The activity cards in the main section of this book provide independent vocabulary-development practice. You can reinforce that learning through a variety of ongoing and special-event activities. Some of these use resource pages that follow this section.

Ask Me About It

Have students devote a section in their journals to interesting words met in reading, in conversations, on TV, and elsewhere. One child might be fascinated by the word *pumpernickel*, while another might want to know about *gaffer* (an electrician working on a movie). Students can share their favorites by giving one-minute presentations, or by writing about their words in the school's daily flyer, or even by giving soapbox orations on the playground during recess.

Book Reports

A powerful way to capture the essence of any book is to zero in on a single word. For example, when reading *Alice's Adventures in Wonderland*, one reader might choose the word "dream" as the key to understanding this classic. Another might focus on "journey." Building a book report on one word takes writers beyond plot rehashing, and challenges them to deal with the deeper issue of a book's theme.

Current Events Word Reports

Have students collect words highlighted in the newspaper or on TV. For example, during an international conflict, they might investigate place names and cultural terms. At election time, they could define campaign jargon. Reports can take such forms as a "Words in the News" bulletin board or a "Weekly Word Roundup" published in the school newspaper.

Curriculum Review Glossaries

Have students prepare mini-dictionaries in which they explain the major words related to a given topic. For example, following a science unit devoted to the moon, a glossary might include: *crater*, *Galileo*, *libration*, *lunar*, *meteor*, *ray*, *rill*, *terminator*, *tide*, and *selenography*. The words could be presented in a word booklet, or could be discussed by a group of "lunar panelists."

Dictionary Tours

To help students become comfortable using a dictionary, have students make presentations in which they focus on specific word entries. After printing an entry on the board or on an overhead slide, the presenter "walks" the class through the key elements of the particular word:

- syllabification
- phonetic spelling
- part of speech label
- multiple meanings
- synonyms and antonyms
- etymologies

You might also include reports on the many resources found in a dictionary, for example, the pronunciation key, world maps, and charts presenting weights and measures.

Enunciation Chalk Talks

Have each student give a short presentation on a tricky-to-pronounce or frequently mispronounced word. You'll find a list of pronunciation puzzlers on page 88. After printing the word on the chalkboard—for example, etc., the student might say something like this:

> The word *etc.* is an abbreviation of a Latin phrase *et cetera* which means "and other things." Notice that the *c* follows the *et*. That's why the word is pronounced *et cetera*. Say it with me now, "et cetera."

A related activity is leading the class in an original or a classic tongue twister.

Tongue Twisters

Ants are antsy.
Bluebirds bluff.
Crickets crackle.
Do donuts delight?
Eels escape.
Fry fresh fritters.
Grow green grass.
Help her heroes.
Ink is icky.
Just jump.
King Kong kicks.
Lick lollies.
Move my map.
Noise annoys.
Open oil oozes.
Please praise prunes.
Quack quickly.
Red rockets roar.
Swim swiftly.
Train tracks tremble.
Unfold umbrellas.
View videos.
Wake wolves.
X-rays are extra.
Yikes, you yodel.
Zebras zigzag.

Etymology Reports

The word *etymology* comes from a Greek word meaning "studying the truth." An etymology is the true, original— meaning of a word. Exploring word origins not only helps students grasp the meaning of specific words. It will also introduce them to fascinating figures in history, and to cultures around the world.

The simplest way to introduce students to etymology is to read aloud short etymologies found in a word origin book. Several are listed in the Reading List. Here's a typical example:

> *Encyclopedia* comes from three Greek words. The first part, *en*, means "in. "The second part *cyclo* means "circle." You'll find *cyclo* in our word bicycle. The third part, *pedia* means "learning." If you put the parts together, you get the idea that an encyclopedia encircles what there is to learn by presenting a wide variety of topics from A to Z.

You might point out that English has borrowed words from scores of languages, especially from French, Greek and Latin.

After you've presented a few etymologies, invite students to choose words and make their own presentations.

Jargon-using Guests

Invite experts to visit your class and discuss words used in their fields. For example, a chess player might explain such words as *castle*, *end game*, and *gambit*. A janitor could explain everything from *hex wrench* to *thermostat*. Guests might include students as well as adults.

Riddle Solving

Divide the class into small groups. Write a word riddle on the chalkboard and challenge each group to find the solution. See Homograph Riddles (page 85), Homonym Riddles (page 86).

Monster Word Mastery

For many students, learning the pronunciation and meaning of big words is a confidence builder. The key is realizing that the largest words are constructed of easy-to-manage syllables. Demonstrate this on the board with a famous mouth-filler like *antidisestablishmentarianism*. Then send students to a collegiate-style dictionary to find their own big words such as *accelerando*, *acquaintanceship*, *autodidactic,* and *neuropathology*. Students can teach the class these words in oral reports or use them as topics for written papers.

Publishing

In the tradition of *New York Times* columnist William Safire, have students write short "word" columns for the school paper on topics such as etymologies, pronunciation tips, fad terms, puns, and riddles. Another idea is to publish picture books about words for younger children.

Rewriting

Editing or rewriting text is an authentic way to develop word mastery. For practice, have students translate idioms (page 87).

Scavenger Hunts

Alone or in groups, students can seek words in the dictionary, in books, or other materials. Examples to look for are:
- five-syllable words
- compounds
- words with Spanish origins
- abbreviations
- homographs
- words with silent letters
- proper nouns
- initial words

Seasonal Words Bulletin Board

Brainstorm words that fit the season, including astronomical terms, holidays, weather phenomena, and names of months. For example, fall words might include *autumn* and *equinox*.

Spelling Mnemonics

Have students create memory-jogging sentences for often mis-spelled words, for example, "Never bel<u>ie</u>ve a <u>lie</u>." Older students might also create a book of spelling tricks for younger children.

Taped Teaching

If you have a tape recorder, have students produce vocabulary-development tapes. These might focus on academic words or they could relate to hobbies and other student interests. Tapes could even focus on pronunciation puzzlers (see page 88). Share the finished tapes with parents or with other classes.

Word Collecting

To interest parents in your vocabulary-building program, set up a word-giveaway booth at open house. If your school has a web site, you could publish a page on which students discuss word origin.

Word Family-Tree Presentations

After students become familiar with the idea of roots and word families (see pages 58-72), they might create poster-size displays or bulletin boards teaching about members of a given family, for example, half a dozen "aster" words. These visual lessons would make valuable displays in hallways or in the library.

Word Games

People with large vocabularies often play word games. What may seem a "mere" amusement, often builds interest in new words and dictionaries Some games lend themselves to large group participation, for example, Boggle, in which players try to find words in a grid:

        b u k p
        r g s t
        i mo b
        v e c e

Others, such as Scrabble and crossword puzzles work best in small groups. Teaching students these games can lead to a lifelong interest in word building.

Activity Log

Name: _____

Date	Topic	Title	Format

Eponyms to Research

America: Amerigo Vespucci
amp: Andre-Marie Ampere
April: Aphrodite
Atlantic Ocean: Atlas
August: Augustus Caesar
bikini: Bikini Atoll
Bolivia: Simon Bolivar
bologna: Bologna
Braille: Louis Braille
Bunsen burner: Robert Bunsen
cardigan: Lord Cardigan
Celsius scale: Anders Celsius
Cheddar:Cheddar
decibel: Alexander G. Bell
derrick: Godfrey Derrick
diesel: Rudolf Diesel
Europe: Europa
Fahrenheit: Gabriel Fahrenheit
Ferris wheel: George Ferris
frankfurter: Frankfurt
Friday: Frigga
Geiger counter: Hans Geiger
graham cracker: S. Graham
guillotine: Joseph Guillotin
guppy: R.J. Lechmere Guppy
hamburger: Hamburg
Hubble telescope:Edwin Hubble
Hudson Bay: Henry Hudson
January: Janus
jeans: Genoa
July: Julius Caesar
June: Juno
leotard: Jules Leotard
Levi's: Levi Strauss

marathon race: Marathon
March: Mars
maverick: Samuel Maverick
May: Maia
megahertz: Heinrich Hertz
Morse Code: Samuel Morse
New York: Duke of York
ohm: Georg Ohm
pants: Pantalone
Pap test: George Papanicolaou
pasteurization: Louis Pasteur
pickles: Willem Beukelz
Rome: Romulus
Roquefort: Roquefort
rugby: Rugby
sandwich: Earl of Sandwich
Saturday: Saturn
saxophone: Antoine Sax
sideburns: Ambrose Burnside
sousaphone: John Philip Sousa
teddy bear: Teddy Roosevelt
Thursday: Thor
Tuesday: Tyr
tuxedo: Tuxedo Park
volt: Alessandro Volta
vulcanization: Vulcan
watt: James Watt
Webster's Dictionary: Noah Webster
Wednesday: Woden

Etymologies

abacus, from Greek, "counting board"

A.M., from *ante meridiem*, Latin words meaning "before noon"

America, named for Amerigo Vespucci, a German geographer

automobile, from the Greek word *autos*, "self," and the Latin word *mobilis*, "movable," in other words, a self-moving vehicle, in contrast with a horse-drawn buggy

balcony, from the Italian word *balcone*, "beam"

barbecue, from Spanish word *barbacoa*, "framework of sticks"

blimp, coined in 1915 by A.D. Cunningham, a British air officer

blurb, coined in 1907 by Gelett Burgess

Bolivia, named for Simon Bolivar, South American leader

bon voyage, a French phrase meaning "good voyage"

breakfast, compound of "break" and "fast"

brunch, blended from <u>br</u>eakfast and <u>l</u>unch

burgle, back formation from *burglar*

bus, clipped from the Latin word *omnibus*, "for all," so named because it transports everyone, in contrast with a private vehicle

capture, from the Latin word *capere*, "to take or seize"

caterpillar, from the Latin words *catta*, "cat" and *pilosus*, "hairy"

ciao, an Italian interjection meaning "hello" or "goodbye"

C.O.D., abbreviation for "cash on delivery"

Columbia, named for Christopher Columbus

congress, from the Latin words *com*, "together" and *gradi*, "walk," in other words, a meeting

cosmonaut, from the Russian word *kosmonaut*, taken from the Greek words *cosmo*, "space" and *nautes*, "sailor"

dandelion, from the French phrase *dent de lion*, "tooth of the lion," referring to the jagged edges of the plant's leaves

denim, from the name of the French town *de Nimes*, where the fabric was invented

diagnose, back formation from *diagnosis*

diesel, named for Rudolf Diesel, the German inventor of this kind of engine

digital, from the Latin word *digitus*, "a finger," useful for counting

donate, back formation from donation

Dr., abbreviation of Doctor

e.g., from the Latin phrase *exempli gratia* meaning "for example"

emote, back formation from *emotion*

e pluribus unum, a Latin phrase meaning "from many, one," in other words, "united"

fiord, from the Norwegian word *fjord*, "narrow passage"

Frisbee, from the name of the Frisbie Pie Company, whose pie tins were used in throwing games

gas, coined by Van Helmont, a sixteenth century Belgian chemist

guillotine, from the name of a French doctor who recommended its use

gung-ho, from Chinese, "working together"

helicopter, from the Greek words *helix*, "spiral," and *ptero*, "wing"

Hudson Bay, named for Henry Hudson, an English explorer

Inc., abbreviation of Incorporated

insect, from the Latin words *in* and *secare*, "to cut" or "divide," so named because an insect's body is divided into three sections

jeep, from G.P. for "general purpose (car)," used in World War II

Jr., abbreviation of Junior

karate, from the Japanese words *kara*, "empty" and *te*, "hand"

ketchup, from the Malay word *kechap*, "fish sauce"

leotard, named after Jules Leotard, a French trapeze artist

library, from the Latin word *liber*, "tree bark," used for writing

mob, clipped from the Latin word *mobilis*, "movable," referring to a crowd of people moving from one place to another

motel, blended from mo<u>tel</u> ho<u>tel</u>

Mr., abbreviation of mister

Mrs., abbreviation of mistress

muscle, from Latin *musculous*, "little mouse," referring to the moving bulge made when a muscle is flexed

o'clock, contraction of the phrase "of the clock"

pajamas, from the Hindi words *pai*, "leg," and *jama*, "garment"

parachute, from the Italian word *para*, "to protect," and the French word *chute*, "a fall," thus, protection in case of a fall

parliament, from the French word *parler*, "to talk"

pediatrician, from the Greek words *paidos*, "child," and *iatros*, "doctor"

P.E., abbreviation of "Physical Education"

petition, from the Latin word *petere*, "to ask"

photograph, from the Greek words *photos*, "light," and *graphos*, "writing"

pickle, named after William Beukel, who developed a method of preserving food in vinegar and brine (salty water)

P.M., abbreviation of the Latin phrase *post meridiem*, "after noon"

port (harbor), from the Latin word *porta*, "a door"

pulsar, blended from pulsing star

radar, blended from radio detecting and ranging

safari, from the Arabic word *safara*, "to travel"

scavenge, back formation from *scavenger*

scuba, from self-contained underwater breathing apparatus

selenography, from the name of the Greek moon goddess, Selene

sonar, from sound navigation and ranging

splatter, blended from splash and spatter

submarine, from the Latin words *sub*, "under," and *mare*, "the sea"

telecast, blended from televise and broadcast

televise, back formation from television

TGIF, initial word for "Thank goodness it's Friday"

tote, from the Kongo (African) word *tota*, "to pick up"

trolley, from the Middle English word *trollen*, to roll

TV, initial word for "television"

UFO, initial word for "unidentified flying object"

UNICEF, from United Nations International Children's Emergency Fund

vocabulary, from the Latin word *vox*, "voice"

volt, named for Alessandro Volta, an Italian scientist who did early electrical experiments

Homograph Riddles

Homographs are two words that are spelled alike but have different meanings. They also may have different pronunciations, for example, "I can <u>use</u> this" and "I have a <u>use</u> for this."

The questions below includes homographs. Explain their meaning by writing an answer that uses synonyms for one or both homographs. The first two have been done as samples.

1. What's a <u>bass</u> that plays a <u>bass</u>?
    It's a fish who plays a stringed instrument.
2. What's a <u>drawer</u> of a <u>drawer</u>?
    That's an artist who makes a picture of a piece of furniture.
3. What's a dove that dove into the water?
4. What does it mean to house people in a house?
5. What does it mean that lead can lead to illness?
6. What does it mean that you can't number the days when your fingers feel number than ice?
7. What does it mean for people to polish their Polish?
8. What are you doing when you present someone with a present?
9. What does it mean if all the rowers row in a row?
10. What does it mean that a sow made it hard to sow seeds?
11. What does it mean to shed tears because of tears in your shirt?
12. What does it mean that it's hard to wind twine in the wind?

Homonym Riddles

Homonyms are words that sound alike. Complete each
sentence below with a pair of homonyms.

1. I saw the big brown _____ run across the _____ ground and then climb
   a tree.

2. _____ careful when approaching a _____ hive.

3. That 10-____ diamond is larger than the ____ I pulled from my garden.

4. The house _____ said the _____ was dry and could be used for storage.

5. Be a _____ and chase the _____ away from the garden.

6. I can't _____ enough money at my job to buy that beautiful antique
   _____.

7. I _____ on a jet with sneezing passengers, and that's how I caught the
   _____.

8. In the country of _____ do chefs use olive oil to _____ their frying
   pans?

9. I cut my _____ as short as the fur of a _____.

10. We _____ the _____ of cows mooing.

11. My voice became _____ after I shouted at my _____ to slow down.

Idioms to Translate

I changed my mind and will not be going.

They got up at the crack of dawn.

My parents raised me to tell the truth.

Please give me a ring tomorrow.

I'm sorry that I let you down.

Suddenly, it dawned on me.

I'm well-suited for this job.

You'll get a kick out of the movie.

This book is right up my alley.

Please help me out with this problem.

I put my foot in my mouth that time.

He failed because his heart wasn't in it.

We're late because we were held up in traffic.

When he sees this mess, he'll raise the roof.

That old building's days are numbered.

My bedroom is a disaster area.

I'm fed up with your excuses.

It's late, so let's hit the hay.

Be here at eight o'clock sharp.

Pronunciation Puzzlers

across
adjective
alms
antennae
arctic
ask
asterisk
athlete
auxiliary
calf
calm
chaise longue
chassis
chemise
cliche
conch
Connecticut
coupon
data
deity
depot
diphtheria
drowned
envelope
electoral
epitome
etc.
extraordinary
facts
February
flutist

forbade
forte
fungi
genuine
gauge
guillotine
handkerchief
herb
human
hygienist
idea
Illinois
insects
interesting
irrelevant
jewelry
kiln
Koran
lackadaisical
length
library
mature
medieval
mischievous
mortgage
negotiate
nuclear
often
palm
pianist
pneumonia

privilege
products
program
project
pronunciation
psalm
pulpit
raspberry
realtor
recognize
sacrilegious
sandwich
schedule
similar
soften
species
strength
succinct
technical
theater
Tuesday
vase
vegetable
vehicle
vice versa
victuals
werewolf
Wednesday
ye
yolk
zoology

Answers

8 Abbreviations

A.M., from *ante meridiem*, Latin words meaning "before noon"
Jr., abbreviation of Junior   **Dr.**, abbreviation of Doctor
Mr., abbreviation of mister   **Inc.**, abbreviation of Incorporated
Mrs., abbreviation of mistress

8 Acronyms

radar, from <u>r</u>adio <u>d</u>etecting <u>and</u> <u>r</u>anging
scuba, from <u>s</u>elf-<u>c</u>ontained <u>u</u>nderwater <u>b</u>reathing <u>a</u>pparatus
sonar, from <u>s</u>ound <u>n</u>avigation <u>a</u>nd <u>r</u>anging
UNICEF, from <u>U</u>nited <u>N</u>ations <u>I</u>nternational <u>C</u>hildren's <u>E</u>mergency <u>F</u>und

11 Anagrams

- ear/are
- hint/thin
- tools/stool/loots
- peal/pale/leap
- redo/rode/doer
- care/race

12 Antonyms

- old/young
- helpful/unhelpful
- noisy/quiet
- expensive/cheap
- always/never
- careful/careless

15 British English

- bangs/fringe
- battery/accumulator
- checkers/draughts
- elevator/lift
- flashlight/torch
- French fries/chips

17 Clipped Words

- <u>bus</u> was clipped from <u>omnibus</u>
- <u>taxi</u> and <u>cab</u> were from <u>taxicab</u>
- <u>pants</u> was clipped from <u>pantaloons</u>
- <u>plane</u> was clipped from <u>airplane</u>
- <u>sub</u> was clipped from <u>submarine</u>
- <u>exam</u> was clipped from <u>examination</u>

18 Compound Words

- ballroom
- eyeball
- notebook
- doorbell
- bookcase
- headache
- sidewalk
- highway

ANSWERS

20 Connotation
- cheap/inexpensive
- skinny/thin
- miser/saver

21 Contractions
- can't/cannot
- you're/you are
- wouldn't/would not
- we're/we are
- I'll/I will
- I would/I'd

21 Contraction Making
- she will/she'll
- did not/didn't
- are not/aren't
- they are/they're
- could not/couldn't
- I would/I'd

22 Digraphs
- lau<u>gh</u> (f)
- <u>wh</u>ale (w)
- <u>sc</u>ience (s)
- h<u>ee</u>l (e)

23 Echoic Names
- cereal: Crick Cracks
- airline: Whoosh
- athletic shoes: Clunk
- carbonated drink: Fizzy

26 Euphemisms
- mess/not neat
- angry/not happy
- lost/misplaced
- stole/borrowed without permission

26 Exaggerations
- amazing: bewildering, as if lost in a maze
- miraculous: of a miracle, something that can't be explained
- awesome: filled with awe (fear, wonder, reverence)
- fabulous: of a fable, something imaginary

27 Gender-free Words
- busboy/table clearer
- mailman/letter carrier
- meter maid/meter checker
- policeman/police officer
- salesman/salesperson
- stewardess/flight attendant

ANSWERS

29 High-tech Words
- hardware: building and repair tools/computer components
- mouse: small rodent/computer control device
- net: woven device to catch things/computers working together

30 Homographs
The <u>seal</u> on my tire is broken. I saw a <u>seal</u> swimming in the ocean.
Because I have a cold, I <u>tire</u> easily. My bike <u>tire</u> has a hole in it.
Don't <u>loaf</u>, work hard. I need a <u>loaf</u> of bread.
I can <u>spell</u> almost any word. TV can put you under a <u>spell</u>.

31 Homonyms
- bare/bear
- right/write
- mined/mind
- whole/hole
- here/hear
- stair/stare
- lone/loan
- red/read
- to/two/too

32 Hyphenated Words
good-natured   good-looking
hard-boiled   well-known
soft-boiled

32 Hyphenation Editing
twenty-third, broken-down, seldom-visited, blue-green, nightmare-causing

33 Idioms
It's raining <u>hard</u>. My friend was <u>happy</u>. I <u>was nearly injured</u>. I'm <u>busy</u>. Don't <u>avoid saying what you're thinking</u>.

34 Interjections
Aha means "I understand."   *Nah* means "No."
Boo means "I don't like it."   *Ouch* means "I hurt myself."
Hmm means "Let me think about it."   *Yeah* means "I agree" or "Yes."
Huh means "I don't understand."   *Yikes* means "I'm scared."

ANSWERS

37 Ladder of Words

activity (most abstract)
game
checkers (least abstract)

food (most abstract)
apple
pippin (least abstract)

38 Metaphors (examples)

<u>Metaphorical sense</u>
I'm the <u>head</u> of my club.
You're a <u>star</u> pitcher.
This plan has three <u>steps</u>.
I <u>flipped</u> when I heard the news.

<u>Older sense</u>
I hurt my <u>head</u>.
That's the brightest <u>star</u> in the sky.
Take three <u>steps</u> and stop.
I <u>flipped</u> the pancake.

41 Onomatopoeia (examples)

- barber shop: Snip Snip
- plumbing: Drip Stoppers
- car repair: Vrooom
- toy: Toot, Clang, and Plink

41 Oxymorons

- You're <u>clearly confused</u>.
- That's a <u>polite insult</u>.
- I <u>quickly slowed</u>.
- He's <u>unbelievably honest</u>.

41 Palindromes

noon, mom, did, redder, eye, wow, toot

43 Prefixes

<u>il</u>legal, <u>im</u>mature, <u>mis</u>spell, <u>pre</u>heat, <u>pre</u>mature, <u>re</u>heat, <u>un</u>clear
il- means "not," pre- means "before"
un- means "opposite" or "reverse"

43 Prefixes That Count

<u>bi</u>cycle, <u>centi</u>meter, <u>centi</u>grade, <u>milli</u>meter, <u>tri</u>angle, <u>tri</u>cycle

44 Pronouns

Because my dog barks, my neighbor hates <u>him</u>.
After I collect the cans, I'll recycle <u>them</u>.

 VOCABULARY START-UPS ©1997 MONDAY MORNING BOOKS, INC.

ANSWERS

46 Puns

The pony is saying two things at once: that it has a husky voice (hoarse) caused by a cold, and that it is a small creature (little horse). The pun works because "hoarse" and "horse" are pronounced alike.

47 Reduplication
- mishmash means "jumble"
- palsy-walsy means "friendly"
- flip-flop means "change belief"
- teeny-weeny means "very small"
- ticky tacky means "poorly made"
- pitter-patter means "tapping"

48 Rhyming Riddles
- not fancy jetliner: plain plane
- overweight bonnet: fat hat
- library robber: book crook
- hour-long melody: long song

50 Sniglets
- foggy breath: <u>breathsmog</u>
- drawing on a fender: <u>carpic</u>
- shrunken bar of soap: <u>slipslop</u>
- extra eraser "stuff": <u>rub-crumbs</u>

50 Spelling Patterns (examples)
- If a noun ends in <u>ry</u> or <u>ly</u>, change the <u>y</u> to <u>ie</u> before adding <u>s</u>.
- If a verb ends with a vowel and a consonant, double the consonant before adding <u>ed</u>.
- If an adjective ends in a <u>y</u>, change the <u>y</u> to <u>i</u> before adding <u>er</u>.

51 Spelling Tricks
- <u>forty</u>
- <u>been</u>
- of<u>ten</u>
- <u>early</u>
- h<u>oa</u>rse
- ins<u>tea</u>d
- bel<u>ie</u>ve
- sep<u>a</u>rate

51 Suffixes
- music/musical   -al   turns the noun into an adjective
- final/finalize   -ize   turns the adjective into a verb
- young/youngster   -ster turns the adjective into a noun

52 Surnames (examples)
- place/River
- job/Cook
- color/Green
- animal/Fox
- object/Hammer
- time/Winter

ANSWERS

52 Syllables
- com pu ter
- doz en
- ex ag ger ate
- in tel li gent
- met ric
- con cen tra tion

53 Syllable Simplification (examples)
- automobile/car
- education/learning
- pedestrians/walkers

53 Syllable Stressing
- CAR rot
- FLASH light
- mis TAKE
- TEL e phone

54 Synonyms (examples)
- animal: beast, creature
- fast: quick, speedy
- friend: buddy, pal
- talk: chat, speak

55 Trademarked Names
- Band-Aid/Bandages
- Kleenex/tissue paper
- Frisbee/disk used in games of throwing and catching

56 Umbrella Words (examples)
buildings: gas station, school, church, factory, department store
foods: tomato, rice, beans, bread, apple, spaghetti
places: street, city, mountain, tunnel, desert, park

58 Vowel Pairs
words that follow the rhyme:
        please, read, sailors, boat, floated, sea, beans
words that don't follow the rhyme:
        book, journey, buy, bread

71 X Words
X can stand for an unknown in a math problem. For example, 8-5 = X
X can stand for a place on a map, as in "X marks the spot."
X is a symbol of affection in a letter.

ANSWERS

85 Homograph Riddles
3.   It's a bird that flew into the water.
4.   It means to give people a place to live in a house.
5.   It means that lead can cause an illness.
6.   It means you can't count the days when your fingers feel numb.
7.   It means improving the way they speak the Polish language.
8.   It means that you give the person a gift.
9.   It means the people in a boat are all lined up.
10.   It means that a big pig got in the way of scattering seeds.
11.   It means to cry because of rips in your shirt.
12.   It means that it's difficult to make a roll of twine when the wind is blowing.

86 Homonym Riddles
1. bear/bare
2. be/bee
3. karat/carrot
4. seller/cellar
5. dear/deer
6. earn/urn
7. flew/flu
8. Greece/grease
9. hair/hare
10. heard/herd
11. hoarse/horse

Reading List

Eponyms
Guppies in Tuxedos by Marvin Terban (Houghton Mifflin, 1988). Scores of stories behind words ranging from hamburger to Scrooge.

Etymologies
What a Funny Thing to Say! by Bernice Kohn (Dial, 1974) Roots, slang, pidgin English, and cliches.

Words: origins of everyday words and phrases by Jane Sarnoff and Reynold Ruffins (Scribners, 1981).

Figures of Speech
It Figures by Marvin Terban (Houghton Mifflin, 1993). Alliteration, metaphor, and onomatopoeia.

Homographs
The Dove Dove: Funny Homograph Riddles by Marvin Terban (Houghton Mifflin, 1988).

What's a Frank Frank? Tasty Homograph Riddles by Giulio Maestro (Houghton Mifflin, 1984).

Homonyms
Eight Ate: Homonym Riddles by Marvin Terban (Houghton Mifflin, 1982).

Funny You Should Ask: How to Make Up Jokes and Riddles by Marvin Terban (Houghton Mifflin, 1992).

Idioms
In a Pickle and Other Funny Idioms by Marvin Terban (Houghton Mifflin, 1983). Stories behind idioms such as "Put the cart before the horse."

Names
Last Names First by Mary Price Lee (Westminster, 1985). Researching names, plus origins of common last names from the millions in the U.S.

Old-fashioned Words
Poplollies and Bellibones: A Celebration of Lost Words by Susan Kelz Sperling (Potter, 1977).

Puns
Remember the A la Mode! Riddles and Puns compiled by Charles Keller (Prentice Hall, 1983).

Rhyming Riddles
The Hink Pink Book by Marilyn Burns (Little, Brown, 1981).

Macho Nacho by Giulio Maestro (Dutton, 1994).

Spelling
Demonic Mnemonics: 800 Spelling Tricks by Murray Suid (Fearon, 1981).

Tongue Twisters
A Twister of Twists, a Tangler of Tongues by Alvin Schwartz (Bantam, 1977).